# Contents

# 1) 45 Years of Peace

**There have been 45 years of peace since the UK joined the then European Economic Community in 1973. It is now over 70 years since the end of WWII, which is the longest period in two millennia that any of the 28 countries that now comprise the EU have not been at war with each other.**

The Nobel Peace Prize was awarded to the European Union for the "successful struggle for peace and reconciliation and for democracy and human rights. The stabilizing part played by the EU has helped to transform…a continent of war to a continent of peace."
*(Source: Norwegian Nobel Committee press release. Oct 2012)*

**"Even Boris Johnson says the EU was 'born of the highest motives – to keep the peace in Europe.'"** *(Source: New Statesman. 9 May 2016)*

Our internal and external security is stronger if we remain in the EU. Is it worth the risk of losing that?

We are now living in a much more dangerous world than when the referendum was called in May 2016. Trump, Putin, Xi, Erdogan, and Kim are all egoistic leaders who have threatened or engaged in military action. Conflict in the Middle East has widened and continues to export terrorism. This is not a conducive geopolitical context for Theresa May's 'Global Britain' foreign policy. William Hague, former Foreign Secretary, in a statement to the House of Lords: "If you are less influential in crafting the overall approach of the EU you end up with less influence in the rest of the world." *(Source: BBC News. 6 July 2017)*

David Davis, our 'Brexit bulldog', accepted the UK's vulnerability as he sought a 'security partnership' with the EU "that allows us to tackle the full range of threats that we face... Pan European cooperation has kept people safe. It has kept people alive. And it has protected the peace."*(Source: rusi.org. Davis' speech at the Royal United Services Institute, 6 June 2018)*

**No hard border in the island of Ireland was one of three original conditions set by the EU in the Brexit talks.**

"The Good Friday Agreement… was thanks in part to Britain & Ireland sitting together in all the EU institutions, discovering mutual respect and forging frequent alliances over four decades. [It] also reassured Irish nationalists that…the border could become all but invisible… Both sides welcomed a flood of money from Brussels to underpin cross-border trade, economic development, jobs and reconciliation."
*(Source: Quentin Peel, InFacts. Irish Problem shows EU is peace project, 27 Feb 2018)*

Northern Ireland voted 56/44 to remain in the referendum. Tony Blair has said he finds it 'absolutely extraordinary' that many unionists in Northern Ireland support Brexit, given its potential consequences for the region's political settlement. *(Source: Belfast Telegraph. 9 Apr 2018)*

"The British government are not at all clear about what their future relationship with the European Union is going to be and they are arguing that they are going to leave the customs union and the single market and that will end up a complete disaster for people here on the island of Ireland…People have got used to peace". - *Gerry Adams* (Source: Interview on the Andrew Marr Show. BBC1, 4 Feb 2018)

**No acceptable solution to the Irish border issue has been found.**

# 2) Easy Air Travel

**Within the EU we have a wider choice of airport, airline, and destination in a competitive market which reduces cost. The EU ensures air travel is appropriately regulated to ensure safety, quality of service, and with minimal documentation.**

In 2017, 287 million passengers used 2.2 million flights at UK airports, growing at rates of 6% and 3% respectively. Two-thirds of passengers fly to/from Europe. *(Source: Civil Aviation Authority. Aviation Trends Q4 2017)*

**European Aviation Safety Agency (EASA)** sets the rules for aviation within the EU & EFTA, certifies operators & aircraft, and monitors compliance. Air traffic control (ATC) is organised around traffic flows and not national air space to ensure safe and efficient utilisation of capacity. *(Source: Eurocontrol)*

"The UK will cease to participate in the EASA and UK licensed airlines will no longer enjoy traffic rights to the EU market." *(Source: ABTA. 3 July 2018)*

Air travel is cheap and easy within the EU.
Is it worth throwing that away?

# Open Skies Agreement

The EU enacted a 'Single European Sky' in 2004 which couples the standardisation of practice and the integration of ATC with single market principles that have enabled the expansion of low–cost travel. It also negotiates for all member states 'open sky' agreements with other nations (eg long-haul flights) defining the terms of access for civil aircraft and especially the landing rights. The most significant of these is with the US. *(Source: ec.europa.eu/transport/modes/air_en)*

"Despite Brexiters' hope that their new best friend, Trump, would cut us some slack, his administration is resisting giving airlines such as British Airways and Virgin Atlantic the same flying rights post-Brexit that they enjoy today as part of US-EU open skies agreement. The UK needs to replace 65 international transport agreements, according to the FT." *(Source: Denis McShane, INfacts.org. 6 March 2018)*

## Passenger rights & protection

"The UK's membership of the EU has given travellers many highly beneficial rights and protections, including visa-free travel and access to free or reduced-cost healthcare via the European Health Insurance Card, which was used over 215,000 times in 2015 by UK citizens... there are no WTO rules for aviation to fall back on if we do not reach a deal." *(Source: Association of British Travel Agents, Brexit for travel & tourism, April 2017)*

## Compensation (for scheduled & package holiday flights)

Legislation specifies levels of compensation for cancelled or delayed flights, missed connections, and being bumped or downgraded. It covers flights from EU airports and from other countries by European airlines. *(Source: UK Civil Aviation Authority. Your rights when you fly. Accessed 7 July 2018)*

## Visa-free travel

Despite the UK not being part of the Schengen Agreement and retaining its border controls, its citizens can travel freely within the EU. "Brits to pay £6 visa to travel to EU countries after Brexit (and) will also have to provide personal details and their criminal history." *(Source: Caroline McGuire, The Sun. 26 April 2018)*

**Consular representation** is provided by other member states where the UK has no embassy. The pound sterling has depreciated by around 10% against both the Euro & US dollar (the currency for aviation fuel) in the two years since the referendum, inflating the cost of airline travel and holidays in the US and Europe.

# 3) Freedom of Movement

@albawhitewolf

**FoM is the right of UK nationals to work, live, retire, take holidays, and otherwise visit any other EU country without restriction or bureaucracy. EU-27 citizens have reciprocal rights. The UK, together with Eire, opted out of the Schengen Agreement which means that border controls remain in place.**

Net migration = long-term(>year) immigration - emigration = 280,000 in 2017, *(estimated by the Office of National Statistics)*. Immigration, has remained stable at 630,000 for the last 3 years, after climbing 25% whilst Theresa May was Home Secretary. Net migration of EU citizens has not been greater than non-EU in the last decade, but has fallen by 90,000 since the referendum, and is now well under half of that with the rest of the world (which the Home Secretary can control). Brits continue to leave rather than return, at around 50,000 annually.

*(Source: ons.gov.uk. Migration Statistics Quarterly Report, July 2018)*

Restricting movement which will damage our prosperity and denies life opportunities for our children. Is it worth it?

3.7 million EU nationals live in the UK; 5.7m from the rest of the world; 1.1m Brits live in the EU-27. EU migrants come mainly for work (70%) and have similar employment rates to UK nationals (80%). 20% of them study. There is widespread agreement amongst economists that net immigration is beneficial because it generates higher GDP, lowers net debt, and improves the dependency ratio – crucial for ageing societies. Even Migration Watch found that, since 1995, "immigrants from the EEA had made a positive fiscal contribution" and especially those who had joined the EU in 2004 (ie Romania & Bulgaria). Gordon Brown, former PM, recently indicated ways the Home Office could, under EU rules, exercise greater control including registration on arrival, removal of EU jobless, and prioritisation of local workers. *(Source: Luke Lythgoe, InFacts. 6 ways to manage migration inside EU, 7 June 2018)*

## The UK is at full employment

In March 2018, half the population of the UK - a record level – were in work, a rise of 628,000 since the referendum. However, only 5% of this increase came from the EU because 65% of the jobs went to UK born & 30% to non-EU citizens granted visas by UK gov't. The unemployment rate in May was 4.2% - the lowest in 43 years. Claimants of 1.4 million compare with vacancies of 824,000 (a figure that excludes agriculture). We have a skills shortage that is most intense in health & social work (133,000). *(Data: Office of National Statistics Table EMP06, VACS02. 15 May 2018)*

## The UK needs migrant workers

Other sectors rely on immigrants: IT, food manufacture, warehousing, hospitality (ie tourism) & agriculture – the last two upon seasonal labour *(source data from ONS)*. Many employers in agriculture urgently want reinstatement of the Seasonal Agricultural Workers Scheme.

"Against a backdrop of low unemployment and an ageing workforce, more than a third of businesses view access to labour supply as a threat to the UK's labour market competitiveness *(CBI comment)*. Employers do not think of themselves as employing EEA migrants because they are cheaper but because EEA workers are higher quality or are prepared to do work that British workers are not."

*(Source: Migration Advisory Committee. Interim Update March 2018)*

# 4) European Medicines Agency

The EMA protects public & animal health by ensuring that all medicines available on the EU market are safe, effective and of high quality. It is responsible for their scientific evaluation, supervision and safety monitoring. The EMA was located in London but in November 2017, because of Brexit, it relocated to Amsterdam taking 900 jobs with it.

"We welcome the Government's stated intention to maintain regulatory alignment with the EMA…it is vital that the UK life sciences sector is able to continue to participate in Europe-wide clinical trials. The UK should seek to continue to be a member of EU funding and research mechanisms such as Horizon 2020; the European Network ENCePP as failure to do so could affect patient safety; the European Database on Medical Devices; Eudravigilance and the Pharmacovigilance Risk Assessment Committee; Euratom (to maintain supply of medical radioisotopes not produced in the UK)." *(Source: House of Commons Health & Social Care committee report, 13 March 2018)*

This is not 'cherry-picking', it's the whole fruit tree! Jeremy Hunt, then Secretary of State for Health refused to divulge his own department's scenario plans to the committee because "publication of what might be called the worst-case scenario could itself have an impact on negotiations".

**European Health Insurance Card** is another EU facility, the benefit of which the government itself says it wants UK citizens to continue to enjoy. The EHIC covers treatment that is medically necessary on the same basis as it would be to a resident of the member state that provides it. It provides peace of mind for Brits that travel in Europe but "those with chronic conditions depend on the card most, since finding cover for their conditions using private insurance is prohibitively expensive." *(Source: M S Cato, InFacts, 5 July 2018)*


The National Health Service has vacancies for 10,000 doctors and 35,000 nurses. Recognising this acute shortage, Sajid Javid, newly-appointed Home Secretary, excluded non-EU medically-trained people from the limit on immigration numbers. *(Source: BBC News, 14 June 2018).* Meanwhile, in the first 12 months after the referendum, 10,000 health workers from the EU have left the NHS *(Source: Guardian, 21 Sept 2017)* and 40% of those remaining are making plans to leave *(Source: BMA annual rep meeting, June 2018).* Dr Sapwell, a delegate, proposed: "Brexit is bad for Britain's health. Let's put that on the side of a big red bus and once we have made that clear, the public should vote on the deal."


The BMA passed the motion to "support the idea of the public having a final say on the Brexit deal. It also voted to oppose Brexit 'as a whole'. The Royal College of Nursing and Royal College of Midwives have already called for a people's vote on the final Brexit deal." *(Source: Luke Lythgoe, InFacts. Why was BBC silent when doctors called for people's vote? 28 June 2018)*


**We are already suffering symptoms of the Brexit vote and the prognosis for the future is far worse. Is it worth sacrificing the health of our nation?**

# 5) Consumer Rights

Consumer Rights are protected by a broad swathe of EU directives to national governments on product safety, digital market, financial services, food safety and labelling, energy efficiency, travel and transport.

In 1975, the EEC defined five fundamental consumer rights: health and safety, protection of economic interests, claim for damages, legal representation, and the right to an education.

"Over the last 40 years, this body of law has grown to encompass around 90 European Directives... [The government cannot] guarantee the UK's continued access to the EU's shared network of agencies, mechanisms and infrastructure that police, secure, develop and underpin consumer rights across the Single Market... The Minister was unable to provide us with any plan." *(Source: House of Lords Committee. Brexit: will consumers be protected? Dec 2017)*

"Consumer policy in recent years has shifted from the technical harmonisation of standards to the recognition of consumer protection as part of the effort to establish a 'Europe for citizens'."

*(Source: European Parliament Policy Overview, September 2015)*

"The government, through the EU (Withdrawal) Bill, has committed to maintaining existing consumer rights. But Brexit still poses risks to our consumer protection and enforcement regimes going forward." *(Source: Citizens Advice. Brexit: the outlook for consumers, July 2018)*

# Recent Examples of EU Driven Rights
## The right to a basic bank account
Many of the poorest in society were denied this essential facility. The Payment Accounts directive April 2014 forced banks to accept requests from all EU citizens.

## Net Neutrality
Is the principle that Internet service providers treat all data on the Internet equally, and not discriminate or charge differentially by user. Article 3 in 2015 puts this principle into practice, unlike in the US where big players can act as 'gatekeepers', or in China where internet content is wholly controlled by the state.

## Roaming Charges
Charges for voice calls, text messages and data downloads across EU were dramatically reduced and then abolished from June 2017.

*(Source: European Consumer Organisation www.beuc.eu. Accessed 10 July 2018)*

## Personal data privacy and empowerment of citizens
The EU's General Data Protection Regulation (GDPR) has the potential to be the new global standard. *(www.consumersinternational.org)*. Effective from 25 May 2018, this came too late for the level of the fine raised by our Data Commissioner on Facebook for data breaches to be penal. *(BBC. Facebook faces £500,000 fine from UK Watchdog, 10 July 2018)*

## Collective legal action against wrongs by big companies
Following the diesel engine emission scandal, this is currently under consultation with member states.

Is it worth reducing the level of protection and restricting its scope to transactions bordered within the UK?

# 6) Ban on Discrimination

BAN ⊘N
DISCRIMINATION
AT WORK

@albawhitewolf

**The European Convention on Human Rights makes it unlawful to discriminate on a wide range of grounds including 'sex, race, colour, language, religion, political or other opinion, national or social origin, association with a national minority, property, birth or other status'. The case law relating to these rights has shown that the term 'other status' includes sexual orientation, illegitimacy, marital status, trade union membership, transsexual status and imprisonment. It can also be used to challenge discrimination on the basis of age or disability.**

*(Source: Article 14, European Convention on Human Rights (ECHR), enshrined into UK Law in the Human Rights Act 1998)*

The ECHR is independent of the EU and is not affected technically by Brexit, but the role of the European Court of Justice as the arbiter in disputes is problematic. The EU Charter of Fundamental Rights was adopted by the European Parliament in 2000 and the Treaty of Lisbon 2009 gave it legal effect, though the UK got a derogation.

Can we trust the UK government to protect our rights?

So the EU Charter "is not part of domestic law on or after exit day... [and] Labour's Keir Starmer has said keeping the charter will be part of his 'six tests'." The EU Charter itself "replicates the rights in the ECHR and adds in some new ones, such as:

- human dignity (including bioethics);
- physical and mental integrity (including personal data);
- conscientious objection, asylum (prohibits human trafficking);
- a range of social and workers' rights, including the right to

fair working conditions, protection against unjustified dismissal, and access to health care, social and housing assistance."

"This means that the European Council, the European Parliament, the European Court of Justice, and any other body or institution of the EU must respect these rights when they are making laws, deciding cases, or acting in their official capacities. Member States (such as the UK) need only respect these rights when they are implementing EU law." *(Source: Hannah Johnson, www.rightsinfo.org, 1 August 2017)*

Back in 2014, Chris Grayling, then Justice Secretary, set out a plan to "Repeal Labour's Human Rights Act [and] break the formal link between British courts and the European Court of Human Rights." *(Source: Conservative Party policy document: Protecting Human Rights in the UK, October 2014)* "In the end, the last Conservative manifesto ruled out repealing or replacing the Human Rights Act, which incorporates the convention in UK law 'while the process of Brexit is under way'." *(Source: Daniel Boffey, The Guardian, 18 June 2018)* This suggests the Act could be repealed after UK withdrawal. Our own Equality Human Rights Commission "believe the Government's plan to exclude the EU Charter from the Brexit Bill will lead to a reduction in rights". *(18 January 2018)* A sign of this intent follows. Under the headline 'Verhofstadt slams May for discrimination against EU citizens in freedom of movement row', The Express quoted the EU Parliament's Brexit representative on 2 February 2018: "PM May's proposal to make a distinction between those arriving before March 2019 and during the transition could lead to discrimination against EU citizens in the UK and UK citizens in the EU. EU citizens contribute to Britain; what kind of message does this send to them?"

**Four weeks later, our Prime Minister backed down.**

# 7) Employee Rights

**PAID HOLIDAYS**

**EQUAL TREATMENT**

**HEALTH & SAFETY**

**TIME OFF**

**PARENTAL LEAVE**

**BLUE**

@albawhitewolf

These are wide ranging in scope, including access to paid annual holidays, improved health and safety protection, rights to unpaid parental leave, rights to time off work for urgent family reasons, equal treatment rights for part-time, fixed-term and agency workers, rights for outsourced workers, and rights for workers' representatives to receive information and be consulted, particularly in the context of restructuring. *(Source: Trades Union Congress (TUC). UK employment rights & the EU, 25 February 2016)*

The European Union will legislate on worker protection in the 'gig' economy during a transition period, which the UK will have to implement. Is it worth the risk of diminished rights for workers after Brexit?

"EU employment law provides a minimum standard below which domestic employment law must not fall. In some cases EU law has entrenched at an international level existing domestic employment rights; for example, rights relating to race discrimination and maternity. In other cases, new rights have been transposed into UK law to comply with emerging EU obligation. These new rights were often resisted by the UK government during EU negotiations: for example, agency workers' rights and limitations on working time."

There is a sizeable body of ECJ case law interpreting EU employment rights, which domestic courts are currently bound to follow. Subject to the provisions of the EU withdrawal arrangements or subsequent trade agreement, withdrawal from the EU would mean that UK employment rights currently guaranteed by EU law would no longer be so guaranteed. In consequence, a post-Brexit government could seek to amend or remove any of these. *(Source: House of Commons Briefing: Brexit: employment law, 10 November 2016)*

**"And let me be absolutely clear: existing workers' legal rights will continue to be guaranteed in law – and they will be guaranteed as long as I am Prime Minister."** *(Theresa May, Conservative Party conference speech, Oct 2016)*

The Government was forced by a parliamentary vote to release a Whitehall impact assessment to MP scrutiny, but only once they had signed some form of non-disclosure. The Dept of Business, Energy & Industrial Strategy was tasked with reviewing ways in which the UK's economy could be boosted post Brexit and identified 'maximising regulatory opportunities'. These relate to EU legislation transferred into British Law by the Withdrawal Bill which could be removed under 'Henry VIII' powers (ie without parliamentary approval). One such opportunity specifically identified is the Working Time Directive. This "limits the time most of us can work in a week to 48 hours, requires staff to be allowed a daily rest of 11 hours, and makes annual leave compulsory."*(Source: Benjamin Kentish, The Independent, 9 February 2018)*

**"We conclude that EU membership continues to deliver wide-ranging protections to UK workers.** *(TUC, February 2016)*

# 8) European Arrest Warrant

@albawhitewolf

**The Arrest Warrant was introduced in 2004, this is a mutual arrangement across EU national crime agencies. In the UK, the Crown Prosecution Service (Procurator Fiscal Service in Scotland) issues warrants on suspects in EU countries and extradition hearings are held in courts in Edinburgh, London, & Belfast to review warrants from other member states and make a judgement.**

"The UK used this procedure to secure return of 178 wanted fugitives from justice in 2016. In the 12 years to 2015, 71,000 warrants were received and 2,440 issued. 12,000 arrests were made in the UK leading to 8,300 extraditions; 1,440 suspects wanted in the UK led to 1,250 being extradited to us." *(Source: National Crime Agency statistics)*

A most famous case was "in 2005 when one of the terrorists involved in the London bombing, Hussain Osman, was brought back from Rome where lawyers were seeking to shelter him from British justice."

It is against the German constitution to hand over one of its citizens to a country outside the EU and "UK's future access to EU databases for DNA, fingerprints and air passenger records – under the so-called Prüm Convention – are being blocked by France, according to reports in The Times. Access to this sensitive intelligence must be 'compatible with EU law', accepting the overarching authority of the European Court of Justice as the ultimate arbiter in case of a legal dispute." *(Source: Denis MacShane, InFacts. Brexit boon for criminal & terrorists, 31May 2018)*

Even our former Chief Brexit negotiator realises this as he seeks a 'security partnership' with the EU. David Davis wants to remain in:-
•       The European arrest warrant that "has brought dangerous people swiftly to justice";
•       Europol that has "prevented drugs and guns ending up on our streets";
•       The European Criminal Records System, and information sharing that "helped stop countless terrorist attacks"
And he says that the UK will contribute to the "costs of programmes we want to remain involved in (and) will respect the remit of the European Court of Justice". *(Source: rusi.org, Davis' speech at the Royal United Services Institute, 6 June 2018)*

Not only are our negotiators 'cherry-picking', they are 'cherry-picking' when their own 'red-lines' can be crossed! Another cherry that the UK government want is the Galileo satellite navigation system (GPS is US) which will be fully operational by 2020. British businesses supplied the central technology but will be excluded from further participation on militarily-sensitive security & encryption components of the system. *(Source: R Speed, The Register, 27 June 2018).*

The UK science minister, Sam Gyimah said: "The government has been clear that our preference is to contribute fully to Galileo as part of a deep security partnership with the EU…By forcing through this vote (unanimously adopted by the EU-27), while excluding UK companies from the contracts on unfounded security grounds, the European Commission has put this at risk". *(quoted in eu-policies.com, 16 June 2018)*

**Our police and intelligence agencies need collaborative arrangements to fight international crime and terrorism. Is it worth risking our nation's security?**

# 9) Climate Change Action

@ albawhitewolf

**The EU has been at the forefront of initiatives to limit global warming since the phenomenon was formally recognised by the UN in 1988. The EU was critical to achieving the (UNFCCC) Kyoto Protocol in 1992, introduced the world's first international emissions trading system in 2005, issues Effort Sharing Decisions and Renewables Energy Directives, and intensified cooperation at the EU-China Summit in May 2018 (especially important after Trump's withdrawal from the UNFCC Paris Agreement of 2015).**

Since the beginning of the Industrial revolution in 1750, the UK has been the fourth largest contributor to global warming (75bn tonnes of $CO_2$), some quarter of US cumulative emissions, & half that of China.. In 2016, China emitted 28%, US 15%, EU 9%, & UK 1% of global total of 36bn tonnes. The UK emission per capita is now comparable to that of China. *(Source: www.OurWorldinData.org, Oxford University)*

The UK's own "Climate Change Act 2008 aims to reduce greenhouse gas emissions by 80% of the 1990 level by 2050. The long-term target is translated into five-year carbon budgets, [those] legislated to date have been made in context of the UK as a member of the EU and must continue to be met, unless revised to say otherwise, after the UK has left the EU. UK greenhouse gas emissions have fallen by 38% since 1990, but the Committee on Climate Change has identified a policy gap to meet the latest carbon budget, stating that current policies are likely to deliver at best around half of the required emissions reduction from 2015–2030. The UK was projected to receive €5.5bn from the EU in the current budget round (2014-2020) to fund projects that support climate change (mostly ERDF & ESF)."

**"Political stability is crucial when dealing with climate change policy".** *(Source: House of Lords Briefing, Leaving EU: UK Climate Change Policy, June 2017)*

The EU emissions trading system is a cornerstone of the EU's policy to combat climate change. The system works by putting a limit on overall emissions from designated installations, which is reduced each year. Within this limit, companies can buy and sell emission allowances as needed. This 'cap-&-trade' approach gives companies the flexibility they need to cut their emissions in the most cost-effective way. The ETS covers (11,000) power stations and manufacturing plants… and aviation activities. In total, around 45% of total EU greenhouse gas emissions are regulated by the EU ETS. (UK has 1,000 installations). *(Source: The Chemical Engineer, 20 July 2018)*

"Membership of the EU had a fundamental impact on environmental legislation in the UK, and withdrawal will affect nearly every aspect of the UK's environmental policy. The UK is leaving the EU, not Europe. Its environment will remain inextricably linked to the environment of Europe. Brexit will also change the means by which the UK can most effectively contribute to international efforts to mitigate climate change." *(Source: House of Lords EU Committee report, 14 February 2017)*

Climate change is excluded from the remit of the proposed post-Brexit green watchdog *(www.climatechangenews.com, 14 May 2018)* and there are concerns that many senior Hard Brexiteers are climate change deniers. *(www.desmog.co.uk, accessed 21 July 2018)*

Is it worth jeopardising progress combating Climate Change?

# 10) Clean Air Quality

@ albawhitewolf

**Clean Air Quality is about what we breathe. And what we breathe is potentially polluted by excessive levels of ozone, nitrogen oxides (NOx), sulphur dioxide ($SO_2$), ammonia ($NH_3$), fine particulate matter (PM2.5), and non-methane volatile organic compounds that damage health, cause or exacerbate respiratory and cardiovascular diseases, and reduce lifespan.**

The Ambient Air Quality directive aims to control concentrations of air pollution within the EU. The Commission sets emission ceilings for each pollutant and requires member states to continually monitor and report the level in major urban conurbations and wider rural zones. Breach of any ceiling requires the national government to implement a plan for its alleviation and ultimately a penalty for inaction. Farming ($NH_3$), transport & energy generation are key emitters of air pollution and the directive also aims to improve fuel quality and promote integrated environmental protection requirements in these sectors. *(Source: www.ec.europa.eu/environment/air/quality & eea. europa.eu/themes/air/ national-emission-ceilings)*

"The complexity and extent of EU environmental law, as transposed into domestic legislation, are such that many stakeholders are now concerned that environmental protections and ambitions will be diminished…. The Minister, Dr Coffey, told us that a lot of the UK's air pollution came from the continent. [His scientific adviser] also emphasised that pollution originating in the UK affected the EU in return, noting that 'prevailing winds tend to take our pollution over to the continent more often than not, so we are a net exporter'."

*(Source: House of Lords, Brexit: environment & climate change report, Feb 2017)*

Outdoor air pollution is contributing to **40,000 early deaths a year** in the UK *(Source: Royal Colleges of Physicians, Paediatrics & Child Health, Feb 2016)*
**More than a thousand nurseries are close to illegal air pollution hotspots** in England & Wales. *(Source: Greenpeace investigation April 2017)*

Sheffield Council, one of 28 authorities non-compliant with EU quality limits for NO2 emissions, launched an air quality strategy. "There is not a tension between cleaner air and a growing economy. Polluted air is a major drain on Sheffield's economy; currently cost-ing around £200m every year. A city with clean air, an efficient public transport system, high levels of public travel and healthier citizens will have a stronger, fairer economy." *(Source: Councillor Scott in Air Quality News 6 December 2017)*

UK has been taken to the European Court of Justice over air pollution. "Levels of nitrogen dioxide, mostly produced by diesel vehicles, have been illegally high since 2010 in the vast majority of urban areas in the UK. The government's latest plan in 2017 was condemned as 'woefully inadequate' by city leaders & 'inexcusable' by doctors. Ministers were forced by UK courts to improve the plan in February, after losing in the high court for the third time to environmental lawyers ClientEarth, and have until the end of 2018 to implement the stricter measures." *(Source: Damian Carrington, The Guardian. 17 May 2018)*

Is it worth risking reducing air quality which will directly impact on the health of British citizens?

# 11) Common Fisheries Policy

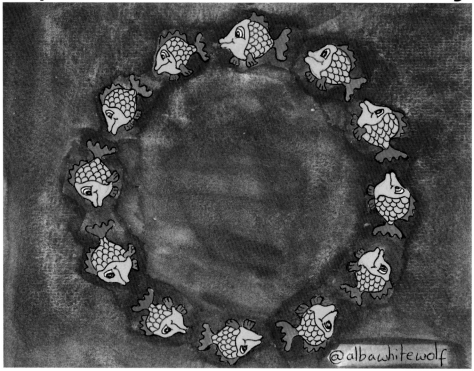

@albawhitewolf

**Ensures fishing and acquaculture within EU waters is environmentally, economically and socially sustainable and applies this principle in negotiating EU member fleet access to international waters. The policy facilitates open access to all bar in-shore waters, but limits each member country's catch based on historic levels of extraction.**

The Common Fisheries Policy reduces competition between fishing fleets of member states in the EU which would otherwise endanger stocks. Stock levels are monitored for their **sustainability** by scientific experts who also recommend technical parameters (eg nets, catching methods). National fisheries ministers mutually agree at Council the annual sizes of catch for commercially-exploited species that are sustainable and the sharing out of that quota amongst member states. The UK enjoys the second largest allocation.

"The number of species within safe biological limits is constant whilst over-fishing of others has been reduced in the ten year period to 2014 – indicating optimal balance between the sustainability of fish stocks and coastal communities." *(Source: EU Scientific, Technical & Economic Committee for Fisheries, March 2016)*

"The Government decides how its EU fishing quota is distributed. If it really cared about the fishing industry, it would ensure these coastal communities with smaller vessels were allowed to fish more. Instead, we have larger foreign vessels being registered in the UK but landing their fish overseas. Brexit won't change that. The Government can but it has done nothing." *(John Prescott, long-time MP for Hull & past Deputy Leader of the Labour Party, in The Mirror. Greed sank the UK's fishing industry, not the EU, 24 March 2018)*

"The majority of fish caught by UK fleets are exported — (71%) mostly to EU Member States. A successful catching industry therefore needs continued market access. The majority of fish consumed in the UK are imported." *(Source: House of Lords Committee report Brexit: Fisheries, Dec 2016)*

The value of exports of fish and shellfish to the EU in 2016 was £1.2bn *(Source: Marine Management Organisation statistics, Sept 2017).* **With no deal, we face tariffs of between 2% and 20%.**

The Royal Navy unsuccessfully fought three cod wars with Iceland between 1949 and 1976. Iceland is not in the EU and not subject to the Common Fisheries Policy. By 2006, North Sea cod was perilously close to extinction but "since then the industry has worked with the Scottish Government and EU Fisheries Council to agree and implement a 'Cod Recovery Plan'" that led to its certification as sustainable by the Marine Stewardship Council in July 2017. *(source: MSC press release)*

"Fisheries constitute a mobile, public and renewable natural resource, which can be accessed by many and consumed only once." Fish do not recognise national jurisdictions and the risk of over-exploitation "necessitates an effective and immediate co-operative relationship in fisheries management with the EU and other neighbouring states". *(Source: House of Lords Committee report. Brexit: Fisheries, Dec 2016)*

**Is it worth damage to our UK fishing industries and risking another Cod War?**

# 12) Rural Development Fund

@albawhitewolf

**The EAFRD helps the rural areas of the EU to meet a wide range of economic, environmental and social challenges. Current priorities are innovation, competitiveness, and sustainability of agriculture, forestry, and rural communities, and adapting ecosystems for climate resilience.**

Over the six year period to 2020, the UK expects to receive €5.2 billion. Each of its four countries decide how to spend their budget allocation and submit a 5-year programme with targets. Rural development funding complements the direct payments farmers receive from the Common Agricultural Policy which are expected to amount to €25bn over the same period.

"A large component of Rural Development Programmes is directed at agri-environment schemes where farmers receive additional payments for practices which especially protect and enhance the environment. The RDP programmes in the UK also support the wider rural economy with priorities relating to tourism, rural broadband, and SMEs."

"EU farm subsidies currently make up around 50-60% of farm income." The UK Government has pledged to maintain the same cash funds as currently for CAP until the end of the current parliament. It has also indicated that it is unlikely to move to any new system of farm support wuntil after 2024.

Environment Secretary Michael Gove has said he is confident of 'building a new economic partnership with the EU' that guarantees tariff-free access for agri-food goods between the UK and EU. [He is also] seeking a flexible migration policy overall and post-Brexit wants to ensure 'access to seasonal agricultural labour'." *(Source: House of Commons Briefing Paper 8218, 28 Jan 2018)*

Many of the uses eligible for EU funding require contributory funding from local sources so as to enhance commitment. As a consequence, case studies can be wrapped up in a banner (eg 'the Growth Deal') which disguises the European contribution. 'LEADER' projects, based on networking through Local Action Groups, have been adopted by the EU since 1991, and are more visible.
Examples include:-

- Small egg farmer local supply-chain management, Lakeland
- 'Bwcabus' on-demand rural bus service, West Wales
- Flood mitigation scheme, Cockermouth
- Farm conversion into small business units, Hertford
- Creation of a nature reserve, Thorley Wash
- Rural Post Office re-establishment, Polesworth
- Milk parlour conversion to a micro-brewery, Northumberland
- Young farmers adoption of robotic milking, Derbyshire
- New stone sculpture micro-business, Bakewell
- Historic conversion into a community library/archive, Strichen
- Ecological restoration of estuaries, Fife

"Leader has clearly demonstrated its efficacy in delivering most of the Axis 3 (social & economic development, tourism & quality of life) measures" and it is recommended that its use is widened from community-based to land-based projects within rural development programmes. *(Source: University of Lincoln. A Review of the Leader Approach, for DEFRA, 2013)*

Is it worth harming the treasured countryside of England, Wales, Scotland, & Northern Ireland?

# 13) Clean Beaches

**Clean Beaches are those from which it is safe for adults to swim and their children to play. The EU standards apply to any bathing waters that are popular and can refer to a river, lake, or reservoir.**

The EU Bathing Water Directive requires that the level of pollution in bathing waters is monitored and assessed, and the public are informed of the quality of the bathing waters. The 'Blue Flag' is the common sign of safety, though accreditation is actually awarded by the Foundation for Environmental Education, based in Denmark. Sewers are the main source of contamination and faecal matter poses a risk to human health. The original EU standards were considerably tightened in 2006 and extended to other forms of pollution.

**Is it worth risking the high standards of water quality in the UK?**

"The UK was branded 'the dirty man of Europe' when it joined the EU, partly due to the polluted state of its beaches. Since then, significant improvements have been made and in, 2016 96.5% of UK bathing waters passed EU standards — announced as the 'best on record' by the Government.  20 sites are still regarded as unsafe." *(Source: Sara Priestley, House of Commons library, 7 Sept 2017)*

"In 1993, a European Court of Justice lawsuit forced the UK government and its newly privatised water industry to clean up infrastructure, and designate sufficient bathing water sites. However, the UK continued discharging raw sewage into the sea until 1998, longer than any other European country." *(Source: Arthur Neslen, The Guardian 23 May 2017)*

We now have cleaner beaches but the rivers in England & Wales are polluted. "There are over 18,000 sewer overflows across England and Wales – and about 90% of them discharge raw sewage (mixed with rainwater) directly into rivers. These discharges are legal but the levels of treatment are not sufficient to protect river health [as it] causes rapid algae growth, starving the river of the oxygen that wildlife needs. WWF is calling on the UK government to act on its commitment to deliver a 'green Brexit' by ensuring at least 75% of our rivers reach 'good ecological status' by 2027. This improvement was set by EU legislation but the UK government isn't remotely on course to achieve it. The situation is getting worse – the number of healthy rivers in England has declined from 27% in 2010 to 14% in 2017." *(Source: World Wildlife Fund investigation, 16 Oct 2017)*

The budget for the UK Environment Agency has been cut by a quarter in real terms since 2010. Michael Gove is the Secretary of State for the Environment, Food, & Rural Affairs and in a statement made in the House of Lords in January 2018, stated that there is an impeccable intellectual case to revamp the Environment Agency "with some of the delivery functions with respect to water & flood prevention being taken on by water companies". *(Source: Abi Kay, Farmers Guardian, 23 Jan 2018)*

**These are the very companies that operate the sewer overflows as a flood prevention measure!**

# 14) Creative Europe

**The European Union Youth Orchestra is an example of film, audio-visual, artists and cultural organisations that benefit from the EU's 'Creative Europe' fund.**

"British orchestras (of which there are 65) have been adept at maximising the return on their public investment through earned income, contributed income, and international touring. Any negative impact to the cultural economy that may result from Brexit will damage their financial viability. [They have] benefited from freedom of movement and access to talent from across the EEA".

*(Source: Association of British Orchestras. Brexit: The Impact, Dec 2017)*

**"The European Union Youth Orchestra** is moving to Italy from London, its home for more than 40 years, in an early example of the cultural fallout from Brexit." Britain's decision in a June 2016 referendum to leave the bloc was a severe blow to many in the arts world, where cross-border collaboration and the ability to tour freely around Europe are valued particularly highly." *(Source: Reuters, 11 Oct 2017)*

"British projects are disproportionately successful in applying for funding and that demand from other EU organisations to work in partnership means that 'the UK has been involved in 44% of projects'."

**European Capital of Culture**, awarded Glasgow in 1990 and Liverpool in 2008, but cities in the UK can no longer be considered. The 'Sage' music hub in Gateshead; 'Home' drama, dance, film, & contemporary Arts centre in Manchester; Falmouth arts campus in Cornwall - all exist because of **EU regional development funds.** Artists gain royalties through Resale Rights; musicians need protection of their Intellectual Property; authors rely on Copyright Law; audio-visual broadcasters on Country of Origin rules; designers & fashion houses on Unregistered Community Design Rights – all shaped in part or in full by EU directives that also provide cross-border enforcement.

"Creative Europe encourages museums and galleries to share their skills, ideas and talent across the EU through its partnership requirement for funding. UK partners in joint projects have been asked to leave or to cease taking a leadership role in projects that would otherwise have benefited the cultural and tourism sectors in the UK.
If the UK were to depart Creative Europe, this would represent a significant blow to the performing arts, museums, galleries, publishing and many other sectors in the creative industries." *(Source: House of Commons committee report. The potential impact of Brexit on the creative industries, tourism and the digital single market, Jan 2018)*

Is it worth diminishing our renowned, dynamic, yet fragile creative & cultural industries?

# 15) ERASMUS+

**Originally a student exchange programme, the scheme has been expanded to provide financial support to education and community organisations to give opportunities to young people and their teachers or facilitators to train, study, volunteer or gain work experience in other primarily EU & EEA nations for up to a year.**

ERASMUS has been a boon to Generations X & Y since it began in 1987 when less than 1,000 students studied abroad each year. In the thirty years since, 600,000 UK citizens have benefitted: 300,000 students; 130,000 teachers & youth workers; 100,000 volunteers & youth exchanges; 60,000 vocational trainers.

Brexit will deny millennials and future generations the opportunity to develop personally, academically, and professionally. Is it worth it?

The current seven-year ERASMUS+ programme which ends in 2020 has a total budget of €14.7 billion. The UK has been allocated almost €1 billion of this, which is likely to assist about 250,000 people, mostly under thirty years of age, obtain experience abroad.

*(Source: Local Government Information Unit/Children's Services Network, Oct 2017)*

Around 43,000 UK/European students each year cross the UK border to attend university, and two-thirds of this movement of people is organised through ERASMUS+. In 2014, Switzerland lost access to the ERASMUS programme when a referendum vote frustrated compliance with the EU principle of freedom of movement. The parliamentary committee on the impact of Brexit on higher education stated that "our evidence was close to unanimous in its support for the positives of Erasmus+" and "continued membership of Erasmus+ would be the best outcome for the UK". *(Source: House of Commons Education Committee Report, April 2017)*

A university student who studied in two EU countries over a year "In an interconnected world, the Erasmus+ programme is so crucial. It opens doors of opportunities for those who are open minded and have a sense of curiosity about the world around them. For me, the programme gave me a life experience that I look back on with pride and that serves as a source of confidence for me as it defines what I can achieve when I set my mind on something. Not to mention the amazing people I have met and the opportunities I would not have otherwise experienced. I hope I will be able to benefit my community and sphere of influence with the skills and lessons learnt so far."

A Welsh school for children with multiple learning difficulties, awarded a double excellent in an Inspection Report for the strategic partnerships developed through staff & pupil visits to three schools. "These experiences give pupils greater self-confidence and improve their self-esteem, communication and social skills. The school's curriculum has been enriched by the wide range of teaching materials that staff and students have brought back from other countries. Staff use these resources well to develop pupils' knowledge and understanding of other cultures and traditions." *(Source: National Agency for the UK Erasmus+ Programme, Dept for Education)*

# 16) Animal Rights

@ albawhitewolf

**to live free from human exploitation and abuse. This includes their use in experiments, as hard labour, being hunted, bred and killed for human consumption, and kept in zoos or for entertainment.**

"Article 13 of the Lisbon Treaty on the Functioning of the EU recognises animals as 'sentient beings' and requires the EU and Member States, when formulating and implementing EU policy on…agriculture and transport, to 'pay full regard to the welfare requirements of animals'." *(Source: House of Lords Committee, Brexit: will consumers be protected? Dec 2017)*

80% of UK animal welfare law originates from the EU *(Source: RSPCA).*

Is it worth animals suffering at the hands of humans by reducing their rights?

Amongst this body of work is the protection of birds and habitats, wildlife trade regulations, pastoral farming standards, zoo licensing, regulation of scientific research, ban on cosmetic products tested on animals, certification framework for veterinary medicines, eradication of invasive species, and the Pet Travel Scheme. In December 2017, AlbaWhiteWolf was able to campaign in Brussels in support of the 'Letters to Europe' project because of her pet passport!

"A number of EU Directives and Regulations contain provisions that relate to the protection and welfare of wild animals, both on land and at sea, and in many respects these go further than international commitments require, setting world-leading precedents for the welfare of wild animals."

"Two factors will be decisive in determining the post-Brexit level of animal welfare for farmed animals: trade issues and the arrangements for farm support payments that replace the EU's Common Agricultural Policy (animal welfare payments)."

"It would not be in the UK's economic interest to allow domestic producers to be undercut by foreign imports, produced to lower animal welfare standards, in a race to the bottom."

"Much animal welfare law is, however, the responsibility of the devolved legislatures...the scope for different parts of the UK to adopt different standards has been relatively small as UK legislation has been required to implement the same substantive requirements set out in EU legislation. UK trade policy post-Brexit is very unlikely to be devolved and therefore the importance of ensuring animals are protected in all areas of trade is likely to remain at a UK level."

"Brexit presents many excellent opportunities to improve the welfare of animals, both in the UK and overseas, in the coming years and decades. We also recognise that Brexit carries risks of dilution and erosion of hard-won animal welfare standards enshrined in EU law."

*(Source: UK Centre for Animal Law / Wildlife & Countryside Link. Brexit: getting the best deal for animals, 16 Jan 2018)*

Our Parliament doesn't appear to have got off to a good start:-
"Unbelievable! Tories vote against transferring into UK law the EU obligation on Govt to pay regard to animal sentience, in favour of a draft Bill that may or may not ever reach Statute Book."

*(Source: Twitter. Caroline Lucas MP, Co-Leader Green Party, 16 Jan 2018)*

# 17) Protected Food Status

**is the recognition of a 'brand' which protects the reputation of regional products, promotes traditional & agricultural activity, and eliminates non-genuine products that mislead consumers. Proof of provenance and breed is increasingly sought by shoppers after miss-selling scandals.**

There are 86 EU certifications of UK products including; Jersey Royal Potatoes; Fenland Celery; Somerset Cider; Whitstable Oysters; Welsh Laverbread; Irish Whisky; Newcastle Brown Ale.

"We could not have hoped for a better boost for our long-term determination to achieve European and world-wide recognition for the special quality of Shetland wool." *(Source: D Rychlik quoted in Shetland Times, 11 Nov 2011)* "The US is lobbying for the rules to be dropped as part of the (post)Brexit trade negotiations. This could mean that rip-off whisky, Shetland wool, wild Scottish salmon could take advantage of Scottish branding." *(Source: Scottish Liberal Democrats campaign, July 2018)*

The much-vaunted trade deal with the US carries broader concerns. The US regulators accept the use of arsenic for weight gain & chlorine for washing chicken, hormone injections in beef cattle, antibiotics for disease control in livestock, and labelling standards that could hide genetic modification. *(Source: Professor Millstone cited in iNews, 27 July 2017).*

The EU bans many of these practices and adopts an approach of preventative hygiene in production rather than ex-post disinfection. Its General Food Law Regulation (2002) is the base for food standards, additives, traceability, trade in feed, and provides a high level of protection for consumers' interests, animal welfare, and environment. The European Food Safety Authority provides scientific advice, risk analyses, and crisis management.

Two of these crises were 'mad cow' (BSE) and foot & mouth diseases that resulted in EU bans on British cattle from 1989-99 and livestock from 2001-3 respectively.

"BSE has been a peculiarly British disaster. Almost all (human) victims of vCJD have been in the UK. Over 170,000 cattle have been diagnosed with BSE here compared with fewer than 1,500 abroad, mostly it would appear traceable to British-sourced animals or infected feed. So far, over 4.7 million British cattle had to be slaughtered, a thriving high-quality cattle and meat export industry has been wiped out, [and] the livelihood of thousands of farmers and businesses damaged." *(Source: Committee of the BSE Inquiry report, October 2000)*

The UK imports roughly half its food consumption, vastly more than it exports, two-third of which comes from the EU with the remainder subject to EU rules & standards on importation. *(Source: DEFRA, 2016)*

"The majority of the industry is likely to welcome the UK government's stated aspiration to negotiate with the EU for 'a common rule book for all goods including agri-food'. The willingness and practicalities of EU states to accept the UK government's stated desire to end 'free movement' and 'the jurisdiction of the (European) Court of Justice' may yet pull the rug from under our government's stated aspiration." *(Source: Kath Dalmeny, Chief Executive of Sustain. 6 July 2018)*

**Is it worth risking our treasured food brands & heritage?**

# 18) Structural and Investment Funds

@albawhitewolf

**S&I funds are grants that promote economic development and social cohesion aimed at reducing disparities between regions (the ERDF) and assist job creation (ESF). Funds for supporting structural adjustment in fisheries (EMFF) and agriculture (EARDF) are covered elsewhere.**

The UK will receive €5.8 billion from the European Regional Development Fund and €4.9bn from the European Social Fund over the current 2014-20 programme. Its priorities are technological innovation, access to ICT (eg 5G wireless), small business competitiveness, and shift to a low-carbon economy. The allocation of funds between projects is a devolved matter but for the 2014-20 programme, the UK government re-assigned monies destined from the EU for England to its sister nations – Liverpool and Sheffield councils unsuccessfully challenged this in court. These cities are in 'transition' regions whose GDP per capita is between 75% & 90% of the EU average – Northern Ireland and the Highlands & Islands of

Scotland are similarly categorised. However, Cornwall and much of Wales have GDP below 75% and EU heavily favours such 'Objective One' regions. (House of Commons Briefing Paper, UK Funding from the EU, 10 January 2018)

# European Investment Bank

"The UK has paid in €3.5 billion in capital to the EIB (16% of the total). Since the Bank's founding, projects in the UK have received €117 billion in loans, 9% of the total lent."

"In 2016, a £700 million loan towards the Thames Tideway Tunnel (is) the largest infrastructure project ever undertaken by the UK water industry...to [prevent] its existing sewers currently overflowing into the Thames on a weekly basis." *(House of Commons briefing paper, European Investment Bank, 16 November 2017)*

# South Yorkshire case study

"The industrial upheavals of the 1980s kicked the stuffing out of communities, and South Yorkshire was amongst the worst hit. History may have proved Margaret Thatcher right in the need for the economy to be administered a strong dose of nasty medicine if the country was to recover from being the sick man of Europe, but the side-effects were horrible...It was the EU that threw a lifeline, supporting a recovery plan put in place by the local authorities in Barnsley, Doncaster, Rotherham and Sheffield, which were faced by the grim fact that without a radical rebirth, the area and its people had no future...And the evidence of the EU's worth is plain to see in the Dearne today, its wastelands now just a memory...We owe the EU a debt of gratitude." (Source: A Vine, What the EU has done for Yorkshire, Yorkshire Post, 21 June 2016)

"The EU Regional Objective One fund that we had (2000 to 2008) has given £1 billion to South Yorkshire...That was used to help rebalance the economy after the collapse of the coal and steel industries" *(Source: Sheffield's business Councillor Bramall quoted by A Evans, The Star, 30 July 2015)*

"Under current plans up to half the funding promised to Sheffield could be clawed back by the government with a stroke of the pen... It would be utterly unacceptable to use Brexit as a way to slash vital funding for building infrastructure, growing businesses and training apprentices." *(Source: LibDem leader Tim Farron quoted by D Hobson, The Star, 10 Oct 2016)*

**Is it worth losing investment in UK infrastructure?**

# 19) Research and Innovation Funds

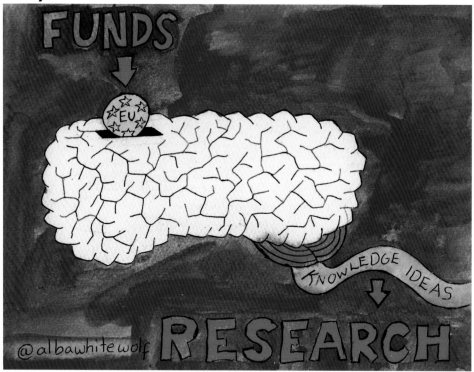

**R&I Funds aim to strengthen the EU's position in science, support industrial innovation, and address major social concerns such as renewable energy, sustainable transport, and ageing populations. The current 7-year framework programme (FP) is 'Horizon 2020' under which project proposals are submitted.**

The UK is a net receiver of EU funding for research. By September 2017, 15% by value of all contracted projects were to UK organisations and 25% by value of those involving universities.

*(Dept for BEIS, Nov 2017)*

"The UK is home to four of the world's top ten universities, and has more Nobel Laureates than any country outside the United States. The UK is second only to Germany in EU project participation, and assurances have been provided about participation in Horizon 2020... the European Parliament could consider UK participation in the (following) EU FP 'as a third country, without permitting net transfer from the EU budget to the UK'. This suggests that the EU might not be content for the UK to be an overall beneficiary after Brexit… It cannot be taken for granted that the UK will retain its status as a science superpower. It is imperative that the migration system for scientists, researchers and scientific technicians recognises the need for mobility." *(House of Commons report: Brexit, science & innovation, 19 March 2018)*

An annex to this report lists 22 European agencies related to science & technology where the UK is currently a member, almost half of which exclude third countries. At the end of May 2018, Theresa May's appeal for continued collaboration met with a provisional view from EU negotiators that the terms would be less generous than third countries under the existing Horizon 2020 programme.

## Euratom

The European Atomic Energy Community (EAEC) regulates the nuclear industry across Europe, a single market for trade in nuclear materials, technology & specialists, and safeguards transportation & disposal of waste. It is legally separate from the EU but has the same membership and is subject to the jurisdiction of the European Court of Justice. *(Source: www.instituteforgovernment.org.uk)*

The UK government formally notified withdrawal from Euratom in March 2017, at the same time as invoking Article 50.

"The United Kingdom would like the option to fully associate ourselves with the excellence-based European science & innovation programmes – including the successor to Horizon 2020 and Euratom R&T (research & training programme). It is in the mutual interest of the UK and the EU that we should do so. Of course such an association would involve an appropriate UK financial contribution, which we would willingly make. In return, we would look to maintain a suitable level of influence in line with that contribution and the benefits we bring." *(Source: Theresa May PM, speech at Jodrell Bank, 21 May 2018. www.gov.uk)*

"Belatedly, the Government seems to be waking up to the fact that breaking our links with European science and innovation programmes would be extremely damaging." *(Source: Ben Bradshaw Labour MP, quoted by www.open-britain.co.uk)*

Is it worth damaging the UK's world class universities?

# 20) Foreign Direct Investment

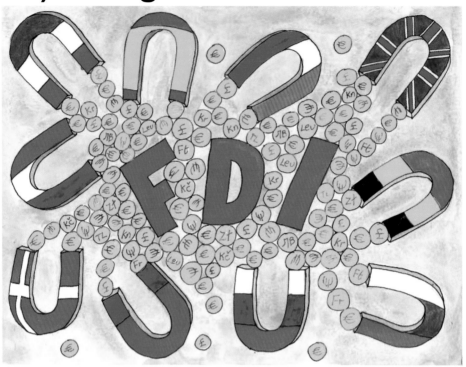

**FDI refers to cross-border investment in business where the financial interest in the company exceeds 10%. Inward investment supports UK manufacturing & service sectors, generating jobs; outbound FDI generates profits for UK investors. Net FDI is the difference and, until this year, reflected a substantial inward flow of funds.**

The UK has consistently attracted more **inward investment** than other EU countries. *(Source: OECD)* The number of projects has fallen for the first time in six years in 2017/18; the number of new jobs has fallen since the referendum & 'safeguarded' jobs halved over the last year. *Source: Dept for International Trade, Inward Investment Results, 26 June 2018)*

"There is a real risk that the UK is treading water and most likely losing out on investment that would help drive future growth… It is unsurprising that access to the European market and the UK's domestic growth are areas of concern, given the Brexit process, but the decline in UK's qualitative appeal is also very striking. The fall in perceptions of stability in the social climate, quality of life, diversity and the political environment show how the UK's image has declined dramatically."

Meanwhile, UK outward investment projects grew by "35% over 2016, leading to the highest-ever UK outflow. Germany...and France were the major recipients as UK businesses appeared to be accelerating their activity to position for the changed environment after Brexit." *(Source: Ernst & Young LLP. EY's Attractiveness Survey UK: In Transition, June 2018)*

The UK's net FDI position fell from £50 to £12.5 billion between 2015 & 2016, the lowest level since comparable records began in 1997. *(source: Office of National Statistics, UK FDI trends & analysis, January 2018).* The EU accounts for half the accumulated stock of inward FDI in the UK of over £1,000,000,000,000 *(Centre for Economic Performance, Brexit Analysis #3)*

## The British Motor Industry

"Investment in Britain's car industry has halved during the past two years with car plants suffering their first fall in output for eight years." Almost 80% of cars made in Britain are exported (56% go to the EU). *(Source: Peter Campbell, Financial Times, 31 Jan 2018)*

"EU tariffs on cars could add at least an annual £2.7bn to imports and £1.8bn to exports. Import tariffs alone could push up the list price of cars imported to the UK from the continent by an average of £1,500." *(Source: Society of Motor Manufacturers & Traders (SMMT). Accessed 6 July 2018)*

'Barrier-free single market access' was a significant motive for Toyota's investment in Derby & North Wales. *(Source: Japan Local Government Centre)* Honda, in Swindon, has warned the government to stay in the Customs Union. Nissan have paused investment in Sunderland. "We must retain tariff and customs-free access to trade and talent with no change to current EU regulations... We have spent around £50bn in the UK in the past five years – with plans for a further £80bn more in the next five. This would be in jeopardy should we be faced with the wrong outcome." *(Source: Ralf Speth, CEO Jaguar Land Rover, 4 July 2018)*

**The UK automotive industry employs close on 1 million people.**
*(SMMT)*

The UK is less attractive for inward investment outside the EU.
Is it worth risking our success?

# 21) Single Market

**The SM is an economic area where barriers to trade between members are removed - stimulating competition, improving efficiency, cutting process, and raising quality through common regulatory & technical standards. The EU single market is an enhanced 'free trade area' because it extends a single freedom (on goods) to 'four freedoms': free movement of goods, services, capital and people. The UK government is currently seeking (as of July 2018) to retain access for goods alone.**

"The single market removes non-tariff barriers to trade, such as differing (product, packaging, labelling & safety) specification... so there is no need to check the conformity of imports at the border."
*(Source: House of Commons Briefing, Brexit: trade aspects, 9 Oct 2017)*

"The three sectors most reliant on the EU market for their inputs are manufacturing at 20% of bought-in costs, health services at 23% (mostly the NHS), social care at 12%, and accommodation & food services at 15%" *(Source: House of Commons Briefing, 1 Aug 2017)*. It is for this reason that the government is planning to stock-pile medicines and food in the event of a 'no-deal' *(Source: Channel 4 News, 25 July 2018).*

Services account for 80% of economic activity in the UK but are excluded from the proposal Theresa May put to the EU. Why is this so? Guy de Jonquieres, former World Trade Editor at the Financial Times believes "that removing barriers to trade in goods – at any rate tariffs – is much simpler than dealing with those affecting services. Another reason is Ireland: keeping goods flowing freely between Britain and the EU reduces the risk of a hard border there. Third, the government may think that the City of London is so big and powerful that business will continue to flock to it after Brexit…no country anywhere has ever managed to conclude trade deals in which services were the only item on the negotiating table." *(Source: InFacts, 20 July 2018)*

**What are the alternatives?** Theresa May wants a bespoke 'partnership' agreement with the EU and is accused of cherry-picking. "Michel Barnier has said that it is not possible to leave the single market and keep all its benefits."
"The EEA option involves considerable access to the single market (but requires the four freedoms) and contributions to EU spending. EEA countries (eg Norway) are outside the EU customs union (and) subject to the EFTA court (not the European Court of Justice)."
"The WTO option would apply in the absence of a negotiated deal with the EU (the 'no deal'). This would involve access to the single market on the least advantageous terms (but with) no contribution to the EU and no free movement of people...the UK will be able to negotiate its own trade deals with other countries (but) at the moment, the UK is bound by a number of WTO trade commitments negotiated by the EU as a whole." These, and any quotas, must be unbundled before the UK can trade under existing deals and "if none of the WTO's 163 members object". *(Source: House of Commons Briefing, Brexit: trade aspects, 9 Oct 2017)*

"The single market is a coherent tapestry of economic and social regulation. Pulling out one strand is very hard to do without changing the whole picture. So far the EU has been consistent in its commitment to keep the single market as it is, with a single set of rules for all." *(Source: M Donnelly, former PS for Dept of Int'l Trade, InFacts, 22 January 2018)*

Is it worth damaging the UK economy?

# 22) Customs Union

The CU is an economic area between countries that has lower or no tariffs (ie taxes) and no quotas (ie volume) on goods traded across internal borders, but has common tariffs and quotas across the union with third countries. The EU's customs union is a free trade area with common rules of origin, regulatory, and product standards which means there are no customs checks at internal borders. The benefits of a customs union normally include increased economic efficiency, less bureaucracy, greater negotiating power on the world stage, protection of industries from dumping and subsidy, and closer political and cultural ties between members.

No deal is not better than a bad deal with the EU, and the best deal is the one we've already got inside the EU.

It is possible to be in a customs union but not the single market (eg Turkey). This is Labour Party policy as it avoids freedom of movement and eases the Irish border problem because origin would not have to be traced. But it would prevent the UK negotiating trade deals with third countries. It is possible to be in the single market but not the customs union (eg Norway). This is government policy but it complicates cross-border transactions: it has tried 'Max Fac', then 'customs partnership', now a 'facilitated customs arrangement' and proposes staying in the customs union as a 'backstop' until a solution to the Irish border can be found! This Hard Brexit approach allows the UK to negotiate trade deals itself and wants to 'inherit' the Free Trade Agreements with 60 countries the EU already has. The UK lacks the bargaining power and the EU is already a relatively low Most-Favoured-Nation tariff applier: its 'simple average' is 5.16% compared to Russia 7%; China 10%; India 13%. The US 3.5% has the most to gain *(Data: World Trade Organisation website).*

"The Prime Minister committed herself to swapping the known benefits of single market membership and the customs union for the hoped-for benefits of a free trade agreement, with a fall-back position of breaking our economic model. That is high risk, and there are big gaps, inconsistencies and unanswered questions in her approach." *(Source: Keir Starmer, Shadow Secretary of State for Exiting the EU, quoted in House of Lords Library Note, 27 Jan 2017)*

In April 2018 the House of Lords rejected government policy to leave the customs union and the House of Commons debated a motion put forward by the chairs of a number of Select Committees which requested the Government to establish "an effective customs union between the two territories." It was defeated in the Commons. *(Source: House of Commons Briefing. Brexit: customs & regulatory arrangements, partially updated 13 July 2018)*

"It would be catastrophic if HMRC's new customs system is not ready in time and if there is no viable fall-back option. The UK's exit from the EU could see the number of customs declarations which HMRC must process each year increase fivefold to 255 million. A failed customs system could therefore lead to huge disruption for businesses, with delays potentially causing massive queues at Dover." *(Source: House of Commons Committee of Public Accounts, Brexit & the future of customs, 13 Nov 2017)*

# 23) Export Market

EXPORT MARKET

INTERNATIONAL STANDARD POSTAGE

PAR AVION

Monsieur: EU
European Boulevard
Brussels, Belgium
Europe

50 EURO    EURO

@albawhitewolf

**Exports are divided between those for goods, on which the UK runs a trade deficit both with EU and with the rest of the world, and services, where it has a healthy surplus in both markets. This distinction is important as the government's proposal is to retain a single market for goods alone. Services comprise 80% of the UK economy**

The EU, taken as a whole is the UK's largest trading partner. In 2017, exports to the EU were £274 billion, or 45% of all UK exports. Wales and the North East of England have the highest dependence on the EU goods market (c60%) and London the lowest (40%). Services account for 40% of UK's exports to the EU, of which financial and business services made up over half.

Trade amongst EU member states is free, but tariffs are paid on goods imported from the rest of the world – the trade-weighted average on agricultural products was 8% in 2014 and for other goods 2%. *(Source: House of Commons Briefing: Statistics on UK-EU Trade, 4 July 2018)*

11% of exports are to the US, 6% to China, and 9% to the 53 countries of the Commonwealth. Since joining the EU in 1973, the ratio of trade to economic output increased from 48% to 67% indicating the UK has become more outward-facing. The EU exported €5 trillion in 2017, 62% between member states. The UK is only the sixth largest exporter with 5.6% of intra-EU trade and has the largest negative trade balance in goods. This is not explained by its trade with the rest of the world. In 2016, the ratio of non-EU exports to non-EU imports in the UK was 68%, compared with Germany (155%), and Ireland (233%). *(Source: Eurostats, ec.europa.eu)* This suggests that UK manufacturers and traders are not making the most of either the EU market or the EU's access to the rest of the world.

The EU has 36 free trade deals with (60) non-EU countries. In 2015, countries with EU trade agreements accounted for over 15% of all British imports and exports. "Without the deals, the UK would be thrust onto World Trade Organisation terms with these countries. Britain's exporters would face costly tariff increases and in some cases more stringent customs checks, with average tariffs levied from 5% to almost 30%. The UK would also have to impose tariffs, raising consumer prices. Britain would lose deeper access to services, as it would no longer participate in the 14 services agreements struck by the EU, including the trade agreement concluded with South Korea." *(Source: Beth Oppenheim, Centre for European Reform, 10 Oct 2017)*

**EU-Japan free trade deal.** The trade agreement is the biggest ever negotiated by the EU and will create an open trade zone covering 600 million people and a third of the world's GDP. The agreement will remove the vast majority of the €1bn of duties paid annually by EU companies exporting to Japan.
"The document we signed today is much more than a trade agreement. It is a statement by two likeminded partners (of) their commitment to uphold the highest standards in areas such as labour, safety, environmental or consumer protection. And what we're saying is that we believe in open, fair and rules-based trade. What we are saying is that a trade agreement is a win-win for the involved parties." *(Source: European Union press release. Quote from the EC President. 17 July 2018)*

Is it worth risking the economic damage to UK trade?

# 24) Prosperity

## Prosperity is traditionally measured by Gross Domestic Product (or GDP).

**An Historic Perspective** "Since 1973, the year in which the UK joined the EU, per capita GDP of the UK economy grew by 103%, exceeding the 97% growth of the US. Within the EU, the UK edged out Germany (99%) & clobbered France (74%). The UK's growth has exceeded the US while tracking it, even since the crisis of 2008. This makes it hard to argue that the EU is dragging the UK down. Alternatively, compare this to the UK's performance during the 'glory days' of the Empire from 1872 to 1914. Back then Britain's per capita growth was only 0.9% per year, in contrast to its robust 2.1% since joining the EU. Since 1974, median income in the UK grew by 79%, in contrast to 16% for the US.

Thus, Britain has had the best of both worlds while a member of the

We shouldn't put politics before prosperity; there is no "Magic Money Tree"; there is no "Brexit Dividend".

EU - not just strong growth, but more equal growth: Boris Johnson recently asserted that the 'EU is a graveyard of low growth'. History is clear: things have gone very well for Britain as a member of the EU." *(Source: INET Oxford. How did the UK economy do since joining the EU? 6 June 2016)* Boris also propagated the infamous £350 million claim on the red bus that heralded the notion of a Brexit dividend. Theresa May has already cashed the dividend by promising increased funding for the NHS from April 2019 *(www.gov.uk PM speech on the NHS, 18 June 2018)*. Vote Leave's bogus claim "is the gross amount before deducting both the rebate won by Margaret Thatcher in 1984 and the money the EU spends in Britain. Adjusting for these, and for the funnelling of some foreign-aid spending via Brussels, the net payment is less than one-third as big, at £17m a day—Britain is only the eighth-largest contributor per head." *(The Economist. The Brexit Briefs, 5 March 2016)*

**A Future Perspective**. Since the referendum the UK has slipped from having the fastest growth of the major G7 economies to the lowest and is now languishing at the bottom of the EU league table. Analysis by the Centre for European Reform "estimates that the UK economy is 2.1% smaller as a result of the vote to leave the EU. The knock-on hit to the public finances is now £440 million a week."

*(Source: John Springford, CER. What's the cost of Brexit so far? 23 June 2018)*

The £sterling has depreciated by 10% against the US dollar and 15% against the Euro since the referendum (as at 26 July 2018), fuelling the rise in UK inflation from 0.5% to 2.5%.

**Economic Impact of Brexit.** The government was forced to reveal the study prepared by its own Brexit department (DExEU) in January 2018 to all MPs once it had been leaked to Buzzfeed. Three plausible scenarios: membership of the EEA, a comprehensive free trade agreement, and no deal requiring WTO rules each projected lower growth over a 15 year period: of 2%, 5%, & 8% respectively. "Almost every sector of the economy… every UK region would be negatively impacted in all the (modelled) scenarios." Independent trade deals with non-EU countries and blocs would compensate less than 1% to economic growth over the long-term.

*(Source: Alberto Nardelli, www.buzzfeed.com , 29 January 2018)*

It is the most optimistic (2%) scenario that was used as a basis for the 'Is It Worth It?' campaigners to 'redecorate' the bus with the revised claim that **Brexit would cost £2,000 million a week!**

# Conclusion - People's Vote

The content of this booklet sets out a positive argument for the EU that has long gone unsaid by the popular press and media. The argument may be biased in favour of Remain, but it is supported by partial & impartial, informed sources and factual data.

The alienation, anger, or frustration with years of austerity resulting from the British public's bail-out of the banks who caused the financial crisis a decade ago is understandable, if wrong-headed. But it was Westminster and not Brussels that preserved the well-being of the City of London at the expense of the rest of the UK.

The expressed motives for Brexit seem to me to have been threefold: economic betterment, regaining sovereignty, or reducing immigration. It should now be evident from this booklet that the prognosis is economic decline, the loss of global influence & fragmentation within the UK, and the need for migrant talent and entrepreneurship for the future wellbeing over our ageing society. **Brexit will not make Great Britain Great Again!**

Just as the government has been incapable of putting a coherent negotiating position to the European Commission, Brexiteers have continually failed to offer coherent arguments for leaving in public debates and fall back upon 'it's the will of the people'. The referendum was called, not because our country had reached a constitutional crossroads, but to lance a boil that had been festering in the Conservative Party for thirty years. Cameron got it wrong: Tory politicians positioned themselves for leadership – and continue to do so – leaving Theresa May as the interim vehicle for delivery – they have the power and will avoid the responsibility.

The 52/48 electoral and 2/4 nation result of the referendum was never an endorsement of a 'hard Brexit', or a 'no deal'. May knew this and so the 'Brexit means Brexit' tautology was born. In the UK, referendum outcomes are constitutionally advisory, not binding, because of the sovereignty of parliament. Government ministers derive their mandate from the Conservative Party manifesto of 2017 which committed them to exiting the single market and customs union, albeit with a vote in both Houses of Parliament on the final agreement. The electorate did not endorse this position as May lost her majority and had to bribe the Democratic Unionists – who themselves acted against the will of the Northern Irish people to remain in the EU – to keep the Tories in power.

**There is therefore still no electoral mandate for Brexit.**

Over 60% of the over 65s voted to leave; over 70% of those aged 18-24 voted to remain. The 16 & 17 year olds who were allowed to vote in the Scottish referendum were denied that right in the UK referendum. 1.5 million teenagers will have turned 18 since the June 2016 vote by the time the deal or no deal is known. My generation, that witnessed the loss of the British Empire and benefitted most from the union in Europe, have turned our backs on our children and grandchildren. We have left a legacy of poorer pension provision, higher education debt, and climate change, and now we are denying them the opportunities in life provided by the EU. I do not trust verbal assurances of the government to give parliament a vote on the deal.

**We need a People's Vote for the people who will bear the consequences of this decision for a generation.**

- Barry Pierce

# Final Word - Positive Narrative about the EU

The two greatest threats to Democracy in the UK are apathy and ignorance: and the biggest challenge for our campaign to Remain in the EU is how to combat these two ills. The Brexit vote was symptomatic of the culture of apathy in the UK. People are disengaged with the political debate and there is a poor level of understanding about the EU. Basic political education is not taught in our schools, and the news media has failed to provide objective, factual information. The British people have been drip-fed a toxic, Eurosceptic narrative by the right-wing press for decades, whilst there has been no discernible positive, pro-European message to challenge it, resulting in a misinformed electorate. When people are then actively lied to by politicians, they don't have the knowledge to challenge what are often very compelling and emotive arguments - resulting in a very dangerous situation for our Democracy. Furthermore, many people vote based purely on emotion, with little heed to the facts necessary to make an informed decision. The Remain campaign in the 2016 referendum failed because of its passionless, facts-based, corporate branded approach which didn't engage the British public. In comparison, Boris, Farage and Gove's emotive propaganda tactics were highly effective and touched people's sense of national identity. In our campaign to stop Brexit, it is crucial that we learn from our past mistakes and use alternative means to engage and communicate with the British people. I believe we do this with a positive narrative about Europe, that generates a sense of pride in our European citizenship and inspires hope and confidence in the UK's future in Europe, in collaborative partnership with the EU27. And we need alternative, varied and creative approaches to communicate our arguments to a wider audience, so that we reach the apathetic and the ignorant. The only positive thing to come out of Brexit is the pro-EU community that has emerged in the UK to fight this mess and we need to support our diverse initiatives to achieve the greatest success possible. Since the Electoral Commission determined that Vote Leave broke the law, there is no doubt of the democratic requirement for another vote, but we need to ensure that when we get a People's Vote on the deal, that we have actually changed people's minds and perceptions of the EU.  - Madeleina Kay

# #24ReasonstoRemain

The purpose of this booklet is to provide key factual information about the EU and likely impacts of Brexit so that readers can make an informed decision in a People's Vote on the final Brexit deal.

The illustrations of the #24ReasonstoRemain aim to create a positive narrative about the EU that communicates the value of our EU membership and how the EU benefits its citizens in their daily lives.

We firmly believe that we are stronger when we work in collaboration with out European partners and we hope this booklet illustrates exactly why Brexit should be democratically stopped through a People's Vote.